DERBYSHIRE DIALECT

A Selection of Words and Anecdotes from
around Derbyshire

Mike Smith

BRADWELL
BOOKS

Published by Bradwell Books
9 Orgreave Close Sheffield S13 9NP
Email: books@bradwellbooks.co.uk

British Library Cataloguing in Publication Data: a catalogue
record for this book is available from the British Library.

1st Edition
ISBN: 9781902674483

Print: Gomer Press, Llandysul, Ceredigion SA44 4JL
Design by: JenksDesign

INTRODUCTION

When I first moved to Derbyshire, almost 40 years ago, I noticed that everyone seemed to be concerned about my health. They would all ask the same question: '*Yaw reet?*' (Are you all right?)

Did I look ill? Did I have a medical condition which was not known to me? These worries disappeared when I realised that the question did not require a reply, but was the normal way of greeting someone, regardless of their physical well-being.

Other questions were equally perplexing. '*Goin' Tidza?*' apparently meant 'Are you going to Tideswell?' Some might call this way of speaking a symptom of laziness, but the locals would see it as economical. Why insert unnecessary words when meaning can be conveyed without them? Why use a complete place-name when the diminutive will suffice?

But, '*by gum*', I could understand some phrases because they were identical to those used in Yorkshire, the county of my birth. Although Derbyshire folk have indeed adopted some of the dialect of neighbouring counties, much of their language is unique, not least that which has been evolved by farmers and miners.

The county's dialect is as characteristic of Derbyshire as its famous hills and dales. Some of that rich verbal heritage is recorded in these pages.

Mike Smith 2013

CONTENTS

A DIALECT DICTIONARY

Regional languages are endangered species, but Derbyshire's dialect is far from extinct. In fact, many of the words and phrases in this extensive vocabulary are still used by folk who live in the county, and not simply by people of advanced years.

In those cases where the meaning of a word or phrase is amplified by a traditional story, the reader is referred to the appropriate chapter in the 'DERBYSHIRE TALES' section of the book.

A

Abaht - about (as in 'abaht time' - long overdue)

Afeered - afraid

Afore - before

Afters - the sweet course in a meal

Aggy - agitated

Agin - again, against

Aht - out (as in 'gone aht' - gone out)

Ails - is wrong with (as in 'What ails thee?' - What is wrong with you?)

Ale-house - pub

All along - always (as in 'I knew a wer reet all along' - I was always convinced I was correct)

An' all - and all (as well)

Ankle-badger (or **ankle-biter**) - hanger-on, sponger

Apostle of the Peak - Rev. William Bagshawe, itinerant preacher

'Appen - perhaps (as in 'appen so' - perhaps so)

Ar - our

'Ark –hark, listen (as in ''ark at that' - listen to that)

Art - are you (as in 'How art?' - How are you?)

Ashford Marble (especially **Black Marble**) - type of limestone found near Ashford-in-the-Water

Athwart - across

Av I eck (or **Av I eck as like**) **-** I've certainly not done so

Aw - all (as in 'Y'aw reet?' - Are you all right?)

Awkin' - carrying

Awkud - awkward

Awluss - always

Aye - yes (I agree)

B

Bacca - tobacco

Back end - autumn, or late in the year (also **Backendish** - feels like autumn weather)

Back-scratcher - someone who seeks favour by behaving sycophantically

Backuds - backwards

Bad-mouth - criticise

Badging hook - large sickle

Badly - ill (as in 'Am reet badly' - I'm very ill)

Bag on - bad mood

Bakewell pudding - a tart made by pouring an egg mixture over a layer of jam in a pastry tray (see 'A Tart Becomes a Pudding')

Balm - yeast

Balmpot - silly person

Battletwig - earwig

Battin' on - going fast

Beestings - milk (colostrum) produced by a cow in late pregnancy

Be said - be told (I've already told you, so no more argument is justified)

Belder - noise a bull makes

Belter - a good one (as in 'It's a belter' - It's really excellent)

Besom - derogatory term for a woman

Bevvy - a drink

Bin - been (as in 'Aster bin?' - Have you been?)

Bit - while (as in 'wait a bit' - wait a while)

Black-jacks - black beetles

Black knobs - alder cones

B

Blart - noise a cow makes
Blaught - bellow (referring to cattle)
Blether (or **Blither**) - talk, reveal
Blubber - cry
Blue John - unique form of fluorspar found in the Castleton area (see 'Sacré Bleu!')
Bobby off - leave quickly
Bodge - mend in a rough and ready way
Bog - toilet
Bog-trotting - jumping from tuft to tuft when crossing sodden moorland
Bole - hearth for burning of lead ore, usually on high land to catch the wind
Bonk - pit-bank or slag heap
Bonser - the village of Bonsall
Booth - shelter for a herdsman (as in Barber Booth, Upper Booth)
Boss-eyed - cross-eyed
Bossunhole - badger hole
Bother - trouble (as in 'Tha's in reet bother' - You're in a lot of trouble)
Bowt - bought
Bradder - the village of Bradwell
Bradder Beaver - a type of miner's helmet produced in Bradwell
Brade - baking shelf
Brass'on - the village of Brassington
Brat - cloth to protect the back from cold weather. Also: a naughty child
Brenners - lead-burners

B

Brew - a cup of tea. Also: 'to make a cup of tea'
Britches - trousers, underwear, knickers
Brizzled - cold
Brow - hillside, steep lane (as in Church Brow)
Buggy - the village of Buxworth (see 'What's in a Name?')
Bunny running - chasing over obstacles
Butties - sandwiches
Button th'lip - button up your lip (be quiet)
Bygones - historical artefacts (Also: '**Let bygones be bygones**' - Don't worry about the past)
By gum - Good heavens!

C

Cack-handed - clumsy (especially when using tools); also: 'left-handed'
Cad - eye-patch
Caded - spoilt
Cadge - borrow or steal
Call - criticise (as in 'Tha's awlus calling us' - You're always criticising me)
Canna - cannot
Can't spit sixpence - thirsty
Careerin' - rushing
Car'son - the village of Carsington
Cart off - take away
Cathedral of the Peak - parish church in the village of Tideswell (see 'Sawyeds of Tidza')
Causey - causeway or pavement

C

'Cept - except

Champion - excellent

Chelly - the village of Chelmorton

Chelp - answer back

Chew - think (as in 'chew it over' - think it over)

Childer - children

Chin cough - whooping cough

Chippa - cheerful

Chivvy - urge to hurry up

Choose how - whatever the circumstances

Chunner (or **Chunter**) - mutter

Clammed (also **Clemmed**) - hungry

Clarts - trousers

Clarty (or **clouty**) - dirty

Clink - prison

Clog - hit (as in 'A'll clog thee one' - I'll hit you)

Close - oppressive (referring to the weather)

Cloth - smack; hit

Cloud - a hill (as in Thorpe Cloud, Hen Cloud)

Clough - valley or small ravine in peat moorland

Clypping - the ceremony of walking around a church in procession

Cob - a bread roll; also means throw

Cobbles - stone setts used for paving a road

Cock-job - work carried out illegally in the workplace

Colley - cauliflower (also **Colleynobs** - Brussels sprouts)

Come a cropper - hurt oneself, especially after falling

Conna - cannot

Coombs - pronunciation of the village of Combs (see 'The Glories of Combs')

C

Cop it - be caught; be punished
Coping stone (or **coper**) - one of the stones placed on the top of a drystone wall
Coss - curse
Coughdrop - someone who makes people laugh
Couldna - could not (as in 'Couldna knock skin off a rice pudding' - very weak)
Cowd - cold
Croaker - doctor
Croggie –a ride taken on the cross-bar of a bike
Crop - batch of new-born lambs
Crozzle - burn to a cinder
Cup o' tea - as in 'my cup of tea' - to my liking
Curfer - curfew (the Curfew Bell in Castleton was called the 'Curfer Bell')
Cussed - cursed
Cut - a canal or railway cutting

D

Dahn - down
Daps - canvas shoes
Darby - pronunciation of the city of Derby (also pronounced '**Dorby**' in some parts of the county)
Dark Peak - the gritstone area of the Peak District
Dation - tub for making oatcakes
Day stone - stone that has been quarried and left to weather
Dead - very (as in 'It wer' dead good' - It was very good)

D

Dead er t'neet - middle of the night

Derby Ram - Derbyshire's most famous folk song (see 'The Finest Ram, Sir')

Derbyshire Neck - the disease of goitre (see 'The Perils of Living on the Bleak Sides of Hills')

Derbyshire's Gretna Green - the village of Peak Forest (see 'Derbyshire's Gretna Green')

Devil's Arse - name given to the Peak Cavern at Castleton

Dew pond - artificial saucer-shaped pond used for watering cattle

Didna - did not

Dipstick - idiot

Dob - hit

Dobber - overtime (at work)

Does ter - do you? (as in 'Does ter lek it?' - Do you like it?)

Dog house – out of favour, in the dog house

Dog in a blanket - roly-poly pudding

Dog shelf - floor

Dollop - lump

Dolly tub - tub for washing clothes

Donkey stone - a whitening stone for steps and windowsills

Doss down - go to sleep or temporarily take up residence

Dousin' - drenching

Dove - water hole (as in the village of Dove Holes)

Down'ards - downwards (also: inhabitants of Ashbourne who live south of Henmore Brook) (see 'Match of the Days')

Downfall - a waterfall (as in Kinder Downfall)

Drag - puff on a cigarette (as in 'Giv' us a drag' - Give me a puff of your cigarette)

D

Draw - place a sheet of newspaper over a fireplace to encourage a coal fire to 'take hold'

Drool - nonsense. Also: '**drool over**' - dote on

Dropped on - taken by surprise

Dry valley - a valley where the river runs underground

Duck –a name given to friends, acquaintances, whether male or female

Dunkin' - dipping a biscuit in tea

Dunna - do not (as in 'I dunna know' - I do not know)

Duster - do you (as in 'What duster want?' - What do you want?)

E

Eck - hell (as in 'What the eck! - What the hell!)

Edge - a high gritstone ridge (as in Curbar Edge)

Eem - the village of Eyam (see 'The Visitation of the Plague')

En'sor - the village of Edensor (see ''Flittin' in En'sor')

Entrance - alleyway between two houses (see also 'Gennel')

Evens - the scores are equal. Can also mean: a score has been settled

Ey up - Affectionate greeting, but can also mean: 'Watch out!'

F

Faberry - gooseberry
Faff - mess about; dither; also **Faffy** - intricate, complicated
Fair to middlin' - keeping reasonably well (healthwise)
Fast - trapped (as in 'I'm stuck fast' - I'm well and truly trapped)
Featherbed moss - peaty tracts on the uplands of the Dark Peak
Feight - fight
Fer - for
Fether - father
Flabbergasted - surprised
Flag - paving stone
Flit - move house (see 'Flittin' in En'sor' and T'Owd Man's Flitted')
Foomart - polecat
Foreigner - a job done in addition to regular employment
Foreign marriages - marriages between couples from outside the parish (see 'Derbyshire's Gretna Green')
Forruds - forwards
Fortnit - fortnight
Fost - first
Frosses - frosts
Fullock - gush of liquid
Furk - scratch

G

Gab - (or **Gabble**) talk (especially: talk too much)

Gaddin' - going out to have a good time

Gaffer - boss

Gallivant - variation of Gaddin'

Gammy - unhealthy, diseased

Gander - look (as in 'Tek a gander at this' - Look at this)

Gansey - a jumper or a sweater

Garlanding Ceremony - a ceremony that takes place in Castleton (see 'Saying it with Wild Flowers')

Gate - a road (especially the route to a place or town), as in Batham Gate

Gawp - stare open-mouthed

Gennel - narrow passage between buildings (see also 'Entrance' and 'Ginnel')

Gerron - move on (also: **Gerron wi' thi** - get on with you - it's difficult to believe you)

Gert - girlfriend

Gi' - give (as in 'Gi' us it' - give it to me)

Gimpy - lame

Ginnel - variation of Gennel (passageway)

Gi' us - Give me

Gleamy - bright

Gleg - look

Glooming - dark and humid

Goaled - a goal is scored in the Ashbourne football game (see 'Match of the Days')

Gob - spit

Gobby - talks too much

Gobsmacked - surprised, amazed

G

Goin' off - happening (as in 'What's goin' off 'ere?' - What's happening here?)
Gollop - eat greedily
Gongoozler - someone who stares
Goster - laugh or stare
Gradely - very good (as in 'reet gradely' - very good indeed)
Grand - great (as in 'reet grand' - really great)
Grange - former monastic land (as in Abney Grange)
Graunch - crunch or grind
Green stone - stone that has only just been quarried
Grinders - teeth (also **Grindle** - grind)
Grough (pronounced 'gruff') - a drainage channel in peat
Groover - a lead-miner
Grove - a trench that is cut into a lead vein
Guide stoops - direction posts placed next to a lane
Gus - goes
Gutser - person who consumes a large amount of food

H

Hag - a bank of peat
Hang t'tab on - listen to a conversation ('tab' is dialect for 'ear')
Hark - listen
Haster - Have you? (as in 'Haster done that?' - Have you done that?)
Have no say - not consulted
Havin' me on - not telling me the truth

H

Heard say - heard it said
Hersel' - herself
Hold yer osses - hold your horses (i.e. wait)
Hole - tunnel or cave (as in Eldon Hole)
Home-spot - place where someone lives
House-side - very large ('he's/she's lek a house-side' - he/she is a very large person)
House-space - living room
How do? - An abbreviation of '**How do you do?**'
Howl - cry loudly
Hug - a type of scrum in Ashbourne's football game (see 'Match of the Days')
Husky-fusky - leap frog
Hutch up - move along

I

I' - in (as in 'i' them days' - in those days)
Idle jacks - peeling skin around fingernails
Ild up - cover up
I'll go to aar house - 'I'll go to our house' - I am surprised
In the pink - in the best of condition, especially 'in the best of health'
Issen - self (missen - myself; thissen - thyself (i.e. yourself))
Is tha? - Are you? (as in 'Is tha goin'?' - Are you going?)

J

Jagger - a person in charge of a train of pack horses
Jar - drink in a pub (as in 'go fer a jar' - go for a drink) (see 'Time Gentlemen Please')
Jiggered - tired
Jiggery-pokery - underhand dealings, trickery
Jitty - narrow lane, alley
Jopson - person
Jowl - push

K

Kape - keep
Kaylied - intoxicated
Keg-handed - left-handed
Keep tha nose owt - keep your nose out (mind your own business)
Ketch - catch
Kibble - bucket for lead ore
Kid (or **Kiddo**) - a male of virtually any age. Also 'our kid' - my sibling
Kindling - firewood
Kine - light, kindle (as in 'kine t'candle' - light the candle)
Kip - sleep or nap
Knacky - capable, handy
Knewd - known (as in 'I knewd all along' - I have always known)
Know yer place - accept the behaviour that is expected of someone in your position
Knows - know (as in 'Tha knows' - You know)

L

Lad - a male of any age
Laddin' - Courting (the female equivalent of wenchin')
Lapping - ladling
Larrop - eat greedily
Larup - cover
Lass - young woman. Also 'our lass' - sister
Lasses - lasts (referring to the lasts used by a cobbler)
Learn - teach (as 'That'll learn thee - That will teach you)
Leet - light
Leg i' bed - leg in bed (as in 'Put yer leg i' bed' - Let's walk arm in arm)
Leg it - run off
Lek - like
Lek - mating display of grouse
Lesh - smooth
Let dog see th' rabbit - move up
Lig - lie
Like - a word added to the end of a sentence in order to give emphasis
Lobscouse - Irish stew
Loosher - slovenly woman
Lost his (her) marbles - can no longer think clearly
Low - a hill (derived from an ancient word for 'mound')
Luggy - knotted up
Lug 'ole - ear hole
Lung - long

M

Made-up - congested (in the throat or nose)

Maiden's garland - (or **virgin's crant**) decoration hung at the funeral of an unmarried woman (see 'Saying it with Paper Flowers')

Mam - mother (as in **Mam Tor** - Mother Mountain, near Castleton)

Manny - bossy

Many a time - often

Mardy - spoilt; grumpy; moody

Mash - make tea

Maudlin' - sentimental

Mawky - overcast

Medder - meadow

Meddlin' - interfering, especially in other people's affairs

Mek - make

Mek do - 'make do' by continuing to use something that really needs replacing

Mek out - decipher (as in 'I can't mek it out' - I can't decipher it)

Mek tracks –'make tracks', meaning **'leave'**

Mester - master

Midden - a place which is untidy or a place where rubbish or 'muck' is stored

Mind thissen - mind yourself (can mean 'make room' or 'be careful')

Missen - myself

Missus - wife

Mizzle - drizzle or light rain

Moggy - cat

M

Monk - in a bad mood or sulking ('Tha's gorra monk on' - You're in a bad mood)
Mony - many (as in 'mony a long year')
Muck up - make a mess, do something incorrectly
Mucky - dirty
Mufter - scarf
Mun - must
Munk - sulk
Munna - mustn't
Myther - pester

N

Naadays - nowadays
Nab - cliff edge. Also means 'steal' or 'get'
Nark - bad temper (as in 'You've got nark on' - You've become bad-tempered)
Na'then - now then (used as a greeting)
Nay - no
Nazzy - bad-tempered
Ne'er - never (also: **Ne'er do well** - a person who is always in trouble)
Neet - night (as in 'Good Neet' - Good night; also **Neets** - night-shift at work)
Neither nowt nor summat - Neither nothing nor something (doesn't amount to much)
Nesh - unable to withstand cold weather
Nipper - child

N

Nivver - never (as in 'nivver mind' - don't worry). Also: 'Well I nivver!' - I am surprised!
Not fit to turn a dog out - the weather is very bad
Not have it - (as in 'A'll not have it' - I'll not tolerate it)
Not particular - don't mind
Nous - understanding
Nowt - nothing (as in 'Tha knows nowt' - You know nothing)
Nuff said - enough said (I don't wish to add anything)

O

Oakey - ice cream
O'er - over
Off-comer - someone who has moved into the area
Ommer ('ammer) - hammer (as in 'Gi' it some ommer' - Really go for it)
Ommocks - feet
On - of (as in 'all on us' - all of us)
One - hit (as in 'A'll give thee one' - I'll hit you)
One in th'eye - to get the better of someone
Oss - horse
Our - belonging to our family (as in 'our lass' –sister; 'our kid' - brother)
Owd - Old
Owd Man - old man; one's father; boss of a family firm; a worked-out mine; guardian spirit of miners (see 'T'Owd Man's Flitted')
Owd - hold (as in 'Owd on a bit')

O

Ower - over
Ower Bill's Mother's - in the distance (as in 'It's black ower Bill's mother's' - It is likely to rain soon)
Ower t'wife's mother's - variation on the above
Owt - anything (also **owt moist** - anything to drink)

P

Pack-up - a lunch-box taken for use in a lunchtime break at work
Parky - cold
Parley - talk
Part - used ironically, as in 'They conna part sing!' - They can't half sing! i.e. they really can sing!
Particular - thorough (as in 'She's not very particular')
Part with - give away
Peaklander - a person who lives in the Peak District
Peltin' dahn - raining heavily
Petalling - pushing petals into damp clay to create a well-dressing picture (see 'Well Dressed' and 'On the Right Lines?')
Petty - a dry closet
Pigged off - annoyed
Piggie - pick at a spot or scab
Pig's ear - mess (as in 'mekin' a reet pig's ear o' that' - You're making a mess of that)
Pike - a prominent summit (as in Eccles Pike)
Pinch - steal
Pine - want

P

Pinfold - an enclosure for holding stray animals
Ploughing wi' dogs - (It's lek ploughing wi' dogs' - It's a job that's been made difficult)
Poached - churned up
Pods - bread dropped in gravy
Poll up - arrive
Pommie (or **Pommy**) - someone who lives in the village of Youlgrave (see 'Pom, Pom, Pom')
Pot - plaster cast
Pots - dishes
Press - now (as in 'up to press' - up to now)
Pressie - gift, present (as in 'a birthday present')
Prick out - use a pin or a needle to mark the outline of a well-dressing picture (see 'Well Dressed' and 'On the Right Lines?')
Privvy - outside toilet
Proper - very (as in 'He's proper poorly')
Puddled - silly or intoxicated
Puddling - mixing clay and water in readiness for well dressing (see 'Well Dressed' and 'On the Right Lines?')
Pumps - soft shoe, plimsolls
Put wood in t' ole - shut the door

Q

Queer - strange (as in 'It wer' reet queer' - It was very strange)

R

Raand - round, around
Rake - a vein of lead ore
Rammel - rubbish
Rapscallion - rogue
Raungin' - reaching
Reckon - think, judge (as in 'Ar reckon he will' - I think he will)
Reet - right (as in 'Are y'aw reet? - Are you all right?); very (as in 'I'm reet sorry' - I'm very sorry)
Reg'lar - often (as in 'He does it reg'lar' - He does it frequently)
Rhymer - a poet
Riddle - sieve
Rindle - a stream that only flows in wet weather
Road - way (as in 'Ger out o't' road' - Get out of my way)
Roarin' - crying
Roaring - brisk (as in 'a roaring trade')
Royal Forest of the Peak - a vast hunting reserve for the Norman Kings (see 'Saying it with Paper Flowers')
Ruck - heap
Ructions - bother
Rum - strange (as in 'rum un' - a strange person)
Rusty - ginger-haired

S

Sam - gather up
Sarnie - sandwich
Saut - salt

S

Sawyeds - inhabitants of Tideswell (see 'Sawyeds of Tidza')

Seed - saw (as in 'I seed him' - I saw him)

Ses - says

Scraitin' - crying

Scrap - fight

Scratchings - pieces of batter available in a chip shop

Scrattin' and scapin' - short of money

Shack-hole - fissure where a river passes underground

Sheeny - coward

Shek - shake, tremble (as in 'A' were all of a shek' - I was trembling)

Shift up - move along

Shimmy - vest

Shimmy up - climb

Shive - slice

Shot - shirt

Shrovie – Shrovetide (see 'Match of the Days')

Shut - rid (as in 'get shut' - get rid)

Shuv - push

Sicky - absence from work due to illness

Sidle - move slowly

Sile dahn (or **Sile it dahn**) - rain heavily

Sin' - since

Sithee - look here

Skank - mean

Sket - fool

Skets - skates (as in 'Get yer skets on' - Hurry up)

Skew-wiff - crooked

Skin a gnat for its hide - tight with money

S

Slarts - insults
Slicken - smooth
Slip-jib - receding chin
Slitherbanks (or **slithery banks**) - scree formed by falling fragments of rock
Slopstone - sink
Slouse - box the ears
Slutter - shuffle
Smarmy - obsequious
Smitten - infatuated, very much in love
Snap - a light lunch
Sneck - door-handle or latch
Snifter - short time
Snuff - easily (as in 'do it like snuff' - do it easily) (see 'It's All Done by Gravity')
Soft - spoilt; stupid (as in 'soft in the head')
Sough (pronounced 'suff') - a drainage channel for a lead mine
Soz - sorry
Spadge - a sparrow
Spidge - chewing gum
Spires - pillars of limestone rock (as in Tissington Spires)
Spout - talk
Sprottling - struggling
Spuggie - sparrow
Squarking - crying; screaming
Starved - very cold
Strikin' - crying
Sucker - ice lolly
Summat - something

S

Sup - drink
Swale - burn old heather in order to encourage new growth; also means 'dry up'
Swallet - the point where a stream disappears underground
Swank - show off, someone who shows off
Swill - wash the door step and the pavement outside a house
Sword - rind of bacon

T

T' (or **Th'**) - the
Tabs - ears
Take a pew - sit down
Tankered - exhausted
Tap dressing - alternative name for well dressing (see 'Well Dressed')
Tappy - near to death
Tarrar - goodbye
Tassle - rascal
Teggies - children's teeth
Tell off - criticise in no uncertain terms
Telt - told
Tek - take
Ter - you (as in 'Does ter lek it?' - Do you like it?); Also - to (as in 'I ay ter' - I have to)
Tha - you (as in 'Does tha know?' - Do you know?)
Tha's - you are

T

That - very (as in 'I were that scared' - I was very scared)
Tha what? - What did you say?
Thee (or **Thi** or **Thou**) - you
Theer - there (see 'It's Just Not Cricket')
Thick as thieves - very closely acquainted and probably sharing secrets
Thine - yours
Think on - take careful note
Thissen - thyself (yourself)
Thotty - thirty
Thowt - thought (as in 'A 'thowt so' - I thought so)
Thrape - hit
Thraped - worn out
Three sheets to t'wind - drunk; disorientated; silly
Throbby - a song thrush
Throng - busy
Throughs - horizontally projecting stones in a drystone wall
Thrutched up - harassed
Thunderclouds - banks of cranesbill flowers
Tickling a trout - catching a trout without using a fishing rod
Tidy - considerable (as in 'a tidy sum of money')
Tidza - the village of Tideswell (see 'Sawyeds of Tidza')
Tin can - coal wagon
Tinsel - the village of Tintwistle
Tin Town - the temporary village erected to house reservoir construction workers
Tip - a spoil heap
'Tis - it is

T

Titfer - hat
Toadstone - local name for an igneous rock
Toadying - being sycophantic
Top o' th' plane - summit of an incline for an industrial railway (see 'It's All Done by Gravity')
Tops (or **topside**) - highest estimate
Tor - a summit, crag or outcrop (as in Mam Tor)
Towd - told
Town - city (also **Townie** - someone who lives, or has lived, in a city)
Tret - treat (as in 'Tret thissen ter a cup a tea'- Treat yourself to a cup of tea)
Trouble at' mill - trouble at home, as well as in the workplace (see Trouble at' Mill)
Tuck - tangle (as in 'I'm in a tuck' - I'm in a tangle)
Tufa - a porous deposit of limestone
Tunes - music
Tup head - a stubborn person
Turn mi bike round - go to the toilet
Turn up the ball - throwing up of the ball to start the Ashbourne football game (see 'Match of the Days')
Twig - understand
Twitchel - alleyway, a lane between gardens
Two penn'orth o' copper - very small (as in 'He's nobbut two penn'orth o' copper')

U

Unwatering - draining a lead mine
Up'ards - upwards (also inhabitants of Ashbourne who live north of Henmore Brook) (see 'Match of the Days')
Urchin - young child, also means a hedgehog
Us - me (as in 'Gi' us it' - Give it to me)

V

Varmint - rogue
Vex - annoy
Visitation of the Plague - when the Great Plague of 1665 came to Eyam from London (see 'The Visitation of the Plague' and 'We All Fall Down')

W

Wakes Week - week reserved for local festivities
Walkin' out - courting
Wang - throw
Wassock - fool
Watter - water
Watterin' hole - public house
Weak in t'head - weak in the head (stupid)
Weasel - very weak tea
Weer - where (as in 'Weer ter been?' - Where have you been?)
Well - very (as in 'well pleased' - very pleased)

W

Well dressing - picture composed of flowers pressed into damp clay (see 'Well Dressed' and 'On the Right Lines?')
Wench - a young lady (also **Wenchin'** - going out with, or chasing after, a young lady)
Were - was (as in 'I were reet glad' - I was very glad);
Werena - was not
Wesh - wash
What's up? - What is wrong?
Whip round - collection of money from a group of people
White Peak - the limestone area of the Peak District
Wi' - with
Wick - nerves (as in 'gets on mi wick' - annoys me)
Wick i'th'head - quick-witted
Winder - window; also **Winder-bottom** - windowsill
Wittle - worry
Wobbie - wasp
Woewer - repairer of drystone walls
Worro mi owd? - Are you all right, mate?
Wunna - won't

Y

Yack - talk incessantly
Y'aw reet? - Are you all right?
Yammer - natter
Yed - head
Yell - cry
Yellow stone - scouring stone for washing stone steps and windowsills

Y

Yer - you; your; you're
Yer on - I'll agree to that
Yonder - there; a long way away (as in 'ower yonder' - over there)
Yorn - yours
Yow'l - you will

Derbyshire Tales

When the writer A A Gill was asked by the deputy editor of *The Sunday Times* what he wanted to do in journalism, he replied: 'I'd like to interview places; to treat a place as if it were a person, to go and listen to it, ask it questions, observe it the way you would interview a politician or a pop star.'

For the past decade, I have been privileged to 'interview' places for monthly features in *Derbyshire Life and Countryside* magazine. The places I have visited have proved to be a source of wonderful stories. Some of their tales are related in this section.

Italics are used where a word from the dialect dictionary appears for the first time in a particular story. They are also used for quotations and poetry.

A Sense of Place

What's in a Name?

In the 1930s, the vicar of Bugsworth, Rev. Towers, and the local schoolmaster, Mr Prescott, decided that the name of their village was embarrassingly ugly, not least because outsiders persisted in calling the place '*Buggy*', so the pair began a campaign to have the name changed. Following a

The change of name from Bugsworth to Buxworth left each of the
station running-in boards with a blank, redundant space

referendum in 1935, the name was officially altered from
Bugsworth to the softer-sounding Buxworth.

In 1999, some villagers decided that they would lobby to have
the name changed back to 'Bugsworth', largely on the
grounds that it would respect the Norman origin of the
village as the 'homestead of the Bugge family'. A second
referendum was held, but the result indicated that sensitivities
were still strong in this corner of Derbyshire, because a clear
majority voted to keep the modern soft-sounding name and

to reject the historical arguments for a return to the original place-name.

If truth be known, the cosmetic change of name from Bugsworth to Buxworth never really succeeded in removing the offending letter 'g'. Derbyshire folk have a marked tendency to use diminutives for place-names. For example, Tideswell is known as '*Tidza*', Chelmorton is called '*Chelly*' and Buxworth is still known as '*Buggy*'.

It's All Done by Gravity

In 1797, the limestone quarries at Dove Holes were linked to the Bugsworth Canal Basin by one of the country's earliest

A ganger on the Peak Forest Tramway braking a wagon by thrusting a pin between the spokes (photo: Picture the Past)

tramways. Horses were used to pull the loaded wagons along the flatter stretches but a revolutionary gravitational railway was employed on the steepest stretch below *Top o' th' Plane* (top of the incline).

Loaded wagons on the down-line were connected by a hemp rope (later replaced by a chain) to empty wagons on the up-line, allowing the weight of the loaded wagons to pull the empty wagons up the hill.

Braking of the descending wagons was achieved in a rather alarming way: a brakeman would ride on the edge of the chassis and lock the wheels by leaning over and thrusting a pin into a socket between the spokes.

In his biography of Joe Marchington ('Chuckling Joe'), a man who lived in the High Peak from 1873 to 1949, Crichton Porteous reports Joe's observation of these brave brakemen: '*It were great t'a watch them, they could do it like snuff.*'

It's Just Not Cricket

As a farmer in the High Peak, Joe was well used to dealing with animals both large and small, but he seems to have had less success in dealing with insects. According to Crichton Porteous, Joe was particularly frustrated when the High Peak suffered from a plague of crickets:

Crichton Porteous (Photo: Derbyshire Life & Countryside)

'They're nasty things,' he said solemnly, 'because yo' never know where they get. An' sing, they conna part sing! Tha sees one on' th' floor an' tries ta stamp on it, a' it's theer, an' theer, an' theer', he said, rapidly stabbing his finger in three different directions. 'Tha meet try six times, a' then never cop it.'

Pom, Pom, Pom

Place-names of many settlements in Derbyshire have evolved over the centuries, but most have arrived at a definitive, accepted form. This is not the case in one village.

Youlgrave Silver Band c1880 with their instruments purchased by the newly-formed Cooperative Society (Photo; The Bugle)

A sign on the A6, between Bakewell and Rowsley, points to the village of Youlgreave, but a finger post at Newhaven, on the Buxton to Ashbourne road, gives directions to Youlegreave. The boundary signs at the entrances to the village name it as Youlgrave.

The village postmaster insists that 'Youlgrave' is the correct version and readily produces his official Post Office map to prove his claim. When it is pointed out to him that the village is marked as 'Youlgreave' on O.S. maps, he contends that cartographers at the Ordnance Survey are incapable of spelling correctly.

Adding yet further to the confusion, the village is known locally as *Pommie* or *Pommy* (here we go again!) and the people who live there are known as *Pommies*.

The origin of these nicknames seems to be connected in some way with the village's Silver Band. The story goes that very few of the musicians who joined the band when instruments were first purchased knew how to play. Consequently, their early repertoire was largely restricted to a repetitive 'Pom, Pom, Pom' as they marched through the village.

This tale has somehow got mixed up with the legend of the 'Pommy Pig', which has become a village symbol. One version has it that the pig would sit on a wall and serenade the band as it passed by, but an alternative version suggests that the pig was so startled by a trumpet blasting out 'Pom, Pom, Pom' that it fell off the wall.

It seems that there is never a single version of any story in Youlgrave (or Youlgreave, or Youlegreave)!

The Finest Ram, Sir

Derby has long been associated with a ram of enormous proportions. Derby County FC is known as 'The Rams'; there is a sculpture of a gargantuan ram in the city centre and the 2nd Battalion of the Mercian Regiment marches behind a real-life ram in their parades.

The city's obsession with this huge creature would seem to stem from a legend popularised in a traditional folk song called *The Derby Ram*. There are many versions of the ditty, but most begin with the same two verses:

As I was going to Darby, Sir,
All on a market day,
I met the finest Ram, Sir,
That ever was fed on hay.

—-

This Ram was fat behind, Sir,
This Ram was fat before,

The Sherwood Foresters marching through Buxton with a ram as
their mascot (Photo: Buxton Advertiser)

This Ram was ten yards high, Sir
Indeed he was no more.

Subsequent verses become ever more exaggerated in their descriptions of the ram, claiming the wool upon his back 'reached up to the sky', the 'wool upon his belly sold for forty thousand pound', the space between his horns was wide enough to build a pulpit, every leg he stood on covered an acre of land, and so on.

Should anyone begin to doubt the accuracy of this portrait, verse 15 makes it clear that the claims are totally accurate:

Indeed, Sir, this is true, Sir,
I was never taught to lie,
And had you been to Darby, Sir,
You'd have seen it as well as I.

The Visitation of the Plague

Eyam (pronounced *Eem*) is still known as the 'Plague Village' and some of its people talk of the terrible *Visitation of the Plague* as if it happened only yesterday and as if they were involved personally in the act of heroic self-sacrifice that took place.

In fact, the story dates back to August 1665, when George Viccars, a tailor who was lodging in an Eyam cottage,

News of the Plague, depicted on a well dressing in Eyam
(Photo: Picture the Past)

received a bale of cloth from his supplier in London. The cloth was damp and contained fleas that were carriers of the Great Plague which was ravaging the capital.

Viccars died within a week of receiving his parcel and five more people who shared his lodgings or lived in neighbouring properties perished from the disease before the end of September. In October, 23 more villagers died.

Catherine Mompesson's Grave in Eyam Churchyard

At this point, the local rector, Rev. William Mompesson, urged the villagers to quarantine themselves from the outside world in order to prevent the spread of the epidemic to neighbouring communities. During the self-imposed quarantine, supplies were left at the perimeter of the village and paid for by coins placed in a trough of sterilising vinegar. When the epidemic finally ended in the late autumn of 1666, over 260 villagers had been wiped out. Rev. Mompesson survived, but his wife, Catherine, who had refused to flee and had chosen to stay loyally by her husband's side, was one of the last to die.

E.L.S. 164-2 William Mompesson, Rector of Eyam during the Plague.

Portrait of William Mompesson, Rector of Eyam at the time of
the Plague (Photo: Picture the Past)

We All Fall Down

It has been suggested by some (but rejected by many) that the nursery rhyme 'Ring a Ring o'Roses' originated at the time of the Great Plague.

Ring a ring o'roses,
A pocket full of posies.
Atishoo! Atishoo!
We all fall down.

Those who suggest that the rhyme is connected with the Great Plague would have us believe that the onset of the infection was marked by a rosy rash on the cheeks, that posies of herbs were carried to counteract the smell of the disease, that sneezing was a symptom of the illness progressing and that falling down dead was the end result.

Although this explanation is not to be sneezed at, there is a ring of poetic licence about it!

Sawyeds of Tidza

Tideswell is one of those Derbyshire villages that are widely known by the diminutive version of their place-names – in this case, *Tidza*.

Anything but Sawyeds - the master woodcarvers William and
Advent (Young Advent) Hunstone of Tideswell
Photo: Michael Hunstone)

The use of shortened place-names is symptomatic of a dislike
of using long words, which is a characteristic trait of
Derbyshire people. If five letters will do, why use nine?

The inhabitants of Tidza are known as *Sawyeds*, a name that
is said to originate from a story about two Tideswell farmers
who found a cow with its head stuck through the bars of a
gate. Rather than sawing through one of the bars to release
the unfortunate animal, they decided to free the cow by
sawing off its head (*yed*).

This description of Tideswellians as *Sawyeds* has been
interpreted by some as an indication that the inhabitants of
this particular village are not very bright!

T'Owd Man's Flitted

T'Owd Man has a number of meanings in Derbyshire dialect. It can refer to one's father or to the boss of a company. It is

T'Owd Man in Wirksworth Church

sometimes used to describe a worked-out mine and it is also the name of the guardian spirit of miners.

The oldest carving of T'Owd Man as a guardian spirit is to be found in St Mary's Church, Wirksworth, but the story of how it *flitted* (moved) there has irked the people of Bonsall for almost 150 years.

The carving was located in St James' Church in Bonsall, before it was removed for safe-keeping by churchwarden John Broxup Coates during the major restoration of 1863. However, when it began to look as if T'Owd Man was in danger of taking up permanent residence in Mr Coates' garden, the carving was rescued from the churchwarden's clutches and taken to St Mary's Church in Wirksworth, where it was promptly built into the wall of the south transept.

Needless to say, the people of Bonsall were not best pleased to find that their special artefact had *flitted* to another village. And they have remained not best pleased ever since. Bonsall's village newspaper carries an image of T'Owd Man on its masthead and is known as *T'Owd Man's Mutterings*. Apparently, this title is a reference to the mutterings that are said to emanate from time to time from the depths of a disused lead mine.

Of course, there are also fairly frequent mutterings from the people of Bonsall about the loss of T'Owd Man to Wirksworth, but rather than mount a vociferous campaign on the lines of Melina Mercouri's demand that the Elgin Marbles be returned to the Parthenon from the British Museum, the villagers seem to have settled for a replica sculpture which they commissioned from Graham Barfield. The sculptor lives in Wirksworth, of all places!

Flittin' in En'sor

Flittin' (moving) took on a whole new meaning when the estate village of Edensor (pronounced *En'sor*) was moved to a new location.

St Peter's Church, Edensor and cottages in different styles
(Photo: Picture the Past)

The demolition began in 1762, when the 4th Duke of Devonshire decided that the view of his estate from Chatsworth House was being rudely interrupted by the sight of Edensor's buildings.

The Duke began demolishing the cottages that were closest to the house, and the removal of the remaining buildings was completed by the 6th Duke in the 1830s, when he asked his head gardener Joseph Paxton and the Derby architect John Robertson to design a new village in a location that would not be visible from the house.

Legend has it that Robertson arrived at Chatsworth with a portfolio containing all his different house designs and asked the Duke to select the one he preferred. As he was too busy at the time to make a carefully considered choice, the Duke flicked through the drawings and simply ordered one of each. As a result, every house in Edensor is different. They range in style from a castellated tower house to an Alpine chalet.

Just one house from the original Edensor has remained in place. It sits in a dip outside the new village and was spared because it was the only cottage that could not be seen from Chatsworth House.

Trouble at' Mill

Having established the first cotton mill in Belper, the Strutt family provided their workers with well-built houses located in a carefully planned residential area, complete with church, school and swimming baths.

Although the Strutts were benevolent to their workers, they were less sympathetic to others. During the eighteenth

Jedediah Strutt, 1788 (Photo: Picture the Past)

century, factory production was replacing home-weaving, which had long provided farming families with a second income, and demonstrations by those who saw their livelihood threatened were becoming commonplace. The Strutts decided to take no chances. They fitted the bridge connecting two of their mills with embrasures from where guns could be fired on any group intent on storming the premises. The gun enclosures are clearly visible to this day.

Time Gentlemen Please

There is ample evidence in Ashover of the suffering inflicted on the village during the Civil War by both Royalists and Roundheads.

Anyone *going for a jar* (going for a drink) at the Crispin Inn will notice a sign bearing the following description: '*Job Wall, the landlord of the inn, withstood the King's troops in the doorway and told them that they should have no more to drink in his house as they had had too much already. But they turned him out and set watch at the door till all the ale was drunk or wasted.*'

The behaviour of Cromwell's troops was even worse. They destroyed the church's records, demolished its windows and used its lead to make bullets. They also reduced nearby Eastwood Hall to ruins!

The Crispin Inn, Ashover in the 1920s (Photo: Picture the Past)

Derbyshire's Gretna Green

In the seventeenth century, the village of Peak Forest was acquired by the Devonshire family and the villagers were provided with a new church by Christiana, Countess of Devonshire.

Because the new building was on Crown land, the vicar, properly known as Principal Officer and Judge of Spiritualities in the Peculiar Court of Peak Forest, was free to grant marriage licences without reference to the bishop of the diocese. Once it became known that he was willing to marry 'anyone, from anywhere, at any time', runaway couples

Choir rehearsing in Peak Forest (Photo: Picture the Past)

from far and wide began making their way to the village. In the seventeenth century, the number of '*foreign marriages*', as they were called, was averaging 60 per year and was proving to be a nice little earner for the vicar.

The hours when foreign marriages could take place were curtailed by the Fleet Marriages Act of 1753 and special licences were prohibited altogether by a further Act of Parliament in 1803. However, subsequent vicars managed to by-pass the legislation by allowing couples to be married in the church if one of the intended had been resident in the village for 15 days immediately prior to the ceremony – a requirement that proved to be a profitable enterprise for the Three Stags Inn (now the Devonshire Arms).

Although the practice of conducting *foreign marriages* has now ceased, Peak Forest is still remembered as *Derbyshire's Gretna Green*.

The Glories of Combs

There is much dispute about the pronunciation of Combs, a picturesque hamlet in the High Peak.

Writing in the 1970s, local historian Marguerite Bellhouse noted that the size of the indigenous population had already been overtaken by the number of *off-comers* (incomers), who could readily be identified by their tendency to call the village '*Coombs*', rather than '*Combs*', as it is written. The village has attracted yet more *off-comers* in the last half century, with the result that almost everyone calls the village '*Coombs*' these days.

Combs is located at the foot of Combs Moss and on the banks of Combs Reservoir. Its considerable charms are celebrated in a local verse:

Combs Lake and Combs Moss from the summit of Eccles Pike

They rave about the glories of Buxton,
In lines that would fill many tomes,
Of the charms and beauties of Dovedale,
But give me the valley of Combs.

It is recorded that one nineteenth-century resident of the market town of Chapel-en-le-Frith, which is situated a mere two miles away, was in the habit of taking his annual holiday in Combs.

Customs and Traditions

Well Dressed

A thanksgiving for a supply of pure water during the Black Death? An expression of gratitude for a productive well in a period of drought? A pagan ceremony which was hijacked by Christians? The origin of the Peak District tradition of *well dressing* is uncertain, but the practice of decorating wells with pictures made from petals pressed onto damp clay is

The Hall Well at Tissington in the 1900s (Photo: Picture the Past)

commonly believed to have begun about 650 years ago in the village of Tissington.

It is known that Tissington suffered from an outbreak of the Black Death in 1348, and the first dressings may well have been a thanksgiving for the end of that terrible epidemic. Over the ensuing years, the custom spread to many other settlements in the *White Peak*. However, Youlgrave's first dressings did not appear until 1829, when they were created to celebrate the arrival of the first piped water in the village – hence the local name of *tap dressings*.

Well dressing has its own rituals and its own language. The pictures are drawn on a large sheet of paper and then transferred to the surface of a bed of damp clay by '*pricking*' their outlines through the paper with a pin or a needle.

The next stage is '*petalling*', which involves filling in the spaces between the outlines by pressing petals and other natural materials, such as leaves, bark and stones, onto the clay.

To avoid everything falling out when the completed picture is hoisted to a vertical position and put on display, the clay is contained in a wooden frame and held in place by nails protruding from the base. Before it can be used, the clay has to be thoroughly mixed with water in a process known as '*puddling*'. This is achieved by a puddler, suitably clad in

Wellington boots, standing in a large metal bath and trampling around in the mixture for some considerable time. Puddling is no longer practised in many villages, because an enterprising firm in Stoke-on-Trent has tapped a lucrative market by selling clay that has already been puddled, thereby striking a blow to tradition, but sparing well-dressers a great deal of soggy labour!

On the Right Lines?

When the people of Chapel-en-le-Frith decided to try their hand at well dressing for the first time in 1995, they sought the advice of an experienced well-dresser, particularly on the vexed subject of outlining.

The dressers of Tissington have always maintained that shapes within the pictures should be outlined to create definition. In some villages, this is achieved by using rows of coffee beans, while other places employ threads of black wool, but Chapel-en-le-Frith's adviser was of a different persuasion.

He said, '*None o' t' best artists use outlining in their pictures, nor should thee. Tuck t'petals into t'clay around each o' t' shapes and tha'll find that yer picture'll be as clear as day.*'

The dressers decided that they would heed this advice for some of the shapes in their composition, but use cloves to

Well dressers in Chapel-en-le-Frith petalling their first dressing

outline less distinct parts of their picture. Over the next day, they watched in horror as oil from the cloves ran into neighbouring petals and discoloured them.

After debating whether they could pass off the effects of this disaster as artistic licence, the dressers realised that they would have to unpick their work and start all over again, being careful to use coffee beans rather than cloves in their second attempt.

When they had completed their picture, the proud dressers decided to invite their adviser to inspect their handiwork. Hoping for some positive strokes, they awaited his verdict. After careful perusal, he said, '*It's not reet bad for a first effort.*' Undeterred by being damned with faint praise, the people of Chapel-en-le-Frith have continued to produce annual well dressings, but they have never again used cloves!

Match of the Days

Ashbourne's Royal Shrovetide ('*Shrovie*') Football Match is no ordinary game of soccer. The goalposts are three miles apart and the pitch is two miles wide; there is no limit to the number of players and the 'pitch' is the shopping streets, *gennels*, streams and culverts of the town. Needless to say, all the shopkeepers nail large protective boards to the front of their premises throughout Shrovetide to prevent damage during the rough-and-tumble.

The match is contested between the *Up'ards* (people who live on the north side of Henmore Brook) and the *Down'ards* (people who live on the south side) and the two teams inevitably find themselves splashing around in the brook at some stage during the match.

Play takes place between 2pm and 10pm on Shrove Tuesday and Ash Wednesday. Other than a prohibition on carrying

Shrovetide football game in Henmore Brook in 1952
(Photo: Picture the Past)

the ball in a bag, a ban on murder and a discouragement of 'unnecessary violence', there are virtually no restrictions on the way the ball can be grabbed from an opponent or moved around. This type of free-for-all football is known as *hugball*, because it proceeds in a series of scrums, or *hugs*, which make a rugby scrum seem like child's play.

Turning up, which starts the game at 2pm on Shrove Tuesday, is carried out by a guest of honour, who throws the ball into the air. The event achieved 'Royal' status in 1928, when the

Prince of Wales turned up the ball and is said to have ended up with a cut on his head. Prince Charles had the honour in 2003, but escaped without injury.

Scoring, or *goaling*, is achieved when a player hits the ball three times against the 'goalpost', or marker board, at one end of the pitch. If a goal is scored after 6pm, play ends for that day, but if goaling takes place before 6pm, a new ball is turned up and play begins again.

New balls are made each year and painted with designs appropriate to the celebrity who turns up the ball. The game originated in Elizabethan times and some historians believe that the very first ball was the severed head of a man who had been executed!

'Tis a Glorious Game

Anyone who believes that football anthems are a modern phenomenon should think again. Ashbourne's famous Royal Shrovetide Football Match is always preceded by a pre-game luncheon and the singing of an anthem, which was composed in 1891:

> *There's a town still plays this glorious game*
> *Tho 'tis but a little spot*
> *And year by year the contest's fought*

Postcard commemorating the turning up of the ball by the
Prince of Wales in 1928

From the field that's called Shaw Croft
Then friend meets friend in friendly strife
The leather for to gain

And they play the Game right manfully,
In snow, sunshine or rain

Chorus:
'Tis a glorious game, deny it who can
That has the pluck of an Englishman
Second Verse:
For a loyal the Game shall ever be

No matter when or where,
And treat that Game as ought but free
Is more than the boldest dare
Through the ups and downs of its chequered life
May the ball still ever roll,
Until by fair and gallant strife
We've reached the treasur'd goal.

Ashbourne's Royal Shrovetide Football Match may be somewhat rougher than games played under the rules of Association Football, but its song is rather less aggressive and a good deal more sporting than those heard on the terraces of many Premiership clubs!

Saying it with Paper Flowers

Ashford-in-the-Water is a pretty place in a beautiful setting on the north bank of the River Wye. The village is known for its sheep-wash enclosure, its picturesque three-arched bridge, its wells and its church, which is modest in size but contains some remarkable monuments.

Above the entrance porch, there is a Norman tympanum with a carving of two animals separated by a tree. Although the identity of the two creatures is not clear, the animal on the left could be a hog or wild boar and that on the right could

Maidens' Garlands, 1933 (Photo: Picture the Past)

be a wolf. Some historians believe that the carving depicts the *Royal Forest of the Peak*, a hunting reserve for the Norman kings, which covered vast swathes of north-west Derbyshire.

The church's other notable survivals hang from the roof of the north aisle. These are four '*maidens' garlands*', or '*virgins' crants*', each of which was hung in the church after being carried in the funeral procession of a betrothed young woman who had died before her wedding day. The garlands have white paper roses attached to a wooden frame, together with a glove or handkerchief which belonged to the young lady.

Originally there were seven garlands, but two had been lost by 1900 and another fell from the roof and broke in 1935. The four remaining garlands were cleaned and restored in 1987 before being re-hung with protective Perspex covers.

The practice of hanging maidens' garlands died out at the beginning of the nineteenth century, with Ashford's most recent *virgin's crant* dating from 1801. Perhaps there has been a lack of suitable subjects since that time!

Saying it with Wild Flowers

May 29th (Charles II's birthday) was declared a national holiday in 1660, with parliament ordering it to be kept as an annual day of thanksgiving for the restoration of the monarchy. It was known as Oak Apple Day in commemoration of the King's escape from Cromwell's forces by hiding in an oak tree near Boscobel House.

Celebrations took place on this special occasion in towns and villages throughout the country until the holiday was abolished in 1859. Despite the removal of official recognition for Oak Apple Day, the village of Castleton has maintained an annual commemoration with its unique *Garlanding Ceremony*.

Garlanding Ceremony in Castleton in the 1950s
(Photo: Picture the Past)

A local man is dressed as Charles II and a huge conical garland of wild flowers is placed over his head and upper body. Accompanied by a local lady dressed as his consort, a troupe of dancers and a band, the 'King' is paraded around the village on horseback, with the procession pausing at each of Castleton's six hostelries for 'refreshment'.

At the end of this pub crawl, the 'King' is relieved of his enormous garland, which is then hoisted to the pinnacle of the church tower. Needless to say, the procession attracts many followers!

Unique to Derbyshire

Sacré Bleu

Below the surface of Treak Cliff (pronounced 'Trek Cliff'), a steep hillside at the head of the Hope Valley, there is a unique deposit of fluorspar that is much prized around the world as a beautiful gemstone.

When the stone is cut and polished, its smooth surface becomes kaleidoscopically patterned with zig-zag bands of blue and yellow – described as *bleu-jaune* in French and freely translated into English as *Blue John*.

Blue John Mine in 1964 (Photo: Picture the Past)

Just why this colourful stone should have been christened by the French, when it is so patently English, is something of a mystery, but the apparent contradiction is perhaps best explained by the fact that some of the earliest Blue John ornaments were cut and polished in France from stone obtained in Derbyshire.

The gemstone's unique occurrence in the hidden depths of a Peak District hillside is an even greater mystery. Some geologists believe that Blue John was formed when hot gaseous material forced its way through cracks in the surface crust to react with the limestone. Others attribute its characteristic coloured banding to a layer of oil that became trapped between a reef of limestone and an overlying layer of gritstone.

Whatever the reason for its formation, Blue John looks wonderful when fashioned into jewellery, vases, bowls, urns, goblets, pendants, miniature pyramids and obelisks. Prized examples of Blue John ornaments are to be found in the Vatican, Windsor Castle and the White House.

Blue John is in short supply these days and the famous Rock Shop in the village of Tideswell sells some pieces made from samples of rock which bear some similarity to Blue John but are actually obtained from Chinese mines.

The French may have named it and the Chinese might be imitating it, but let us not forget that genuine Blue John is unique to Derbyshire and to one particular hillside just beyond the village of Castleton.

A Tart Becomes a Pudding

The story of the making of the first *Bakewell Pudding* (no one in Derbyshire would dream of calling it Bakewell Tart!) is a classic tale of a recipe created by chance.

A special Bakewell Pudding being prepared for the Festival of National Parks (Photo: Picture the Past)

The story goes that a group of noblemen who were visiting the White Horse Inn in Bakewell (now the Rutland Arms Hotel) asked if they could be served a strawberry tart for pudding. The cook misunderstood the instructions given to her by the mistress of the hotel and spread egg mixture on top of the jam, rather than stirring it into the pastry. Instead of attracting complaints from the diners, the accidental dish was an instant hit.

Mrs Wilson, the wife of a Bakewell candle-maker, acquired the recipe for the new pudding and immediately realised its commercial possibilities. She began selling the delicacy from her husband's candle shop and claimed that it contained a secret ingredient known only to herself.

Mrs Wilson knew that her clever ploy was working a treat when she noticed that her customers were much more inclined to wax lyrical about her puddings than about her husband's candles. The shop was transformed into the Bakewell Pudding Shop and began to attract customers from far and wide.

The Old Original Bakewell Pudding Shop is still a magnet for visitors to the town, although it has now been joined by some other shops claiming to have unique access to the original recipe. But, no matter: there is a spirit of cooperation among Bakewell's shopkeepers and all are happy to cash in on the fame of a pudding that was born in the town as the result of a happy accident.

The Perils of Living on the Bleak Sides of Hills

In the eighteenth and nineteenth centuries, the condition of goitre, or swelling of the neck, was so common in the East Midlands, and Derbyshire in particular, that it became known as '*Derbyshire Neck*'.

Winter in the High Peak (Photo: F B Hills)

Writing in 1769, Mr Prosser described the condition as: '*A tumour arising on the fore-part of the neck. It generally occurs somewhere betwixt the age of eight and twelve years, and continues to increase for three, four or five years.*'

Mr Prosser went on to describe the tumour's rather grotesque appearance: '*It occupies the whole of the front neck, as the whole thyroid gland here is generally enlarged, but is rather pendulous in form, not unlike the flap or dew-cap of a turkey cock's neck.*'

Not surprisingly, sufferers, who were almost invariably female, were not only embarrassed by their appearance, but also had great difficulty in breathing, particularly when walking quickly or tackling Derbyshire's hills.

For many years it was thought that the condition was hereditary among certain families in the East Midlands, but one doctor suggested that the swelling was caused by '*living on the bleak sides of hills*'.

It is now known that goitre is most commonly caused by a lack of iodine in the diet and tends to occur in regions where the soil is deficient in iodine. It is easily counteracted by consuming iodised salt or products rich in kelp (seaweed).

Thanks to this advance in medical knowledge, the county's much maligned weather has been exonerated!

Select Bibliography

Books on Derbyshire Dialect

Holland, Philip F., *Words of the White Peak*, Anecdotes Publishing (2008)

Scollins, R. and Titford, J., *Ey Up Mi Duck!*, Countryside Books (2000)

Wright, Pete, *The Derbyshire Drawl*, Dalesman Books (1977)

Internet sites concerned with Derbyshire dialect

BBC Radio Derby: www.bbc.co.uk/radioderby (includes contributions from visitors to the site)

University of Derby, 'Saving the Dying Derbyshire Dialect?': www.derby.ac.uk/news/saving-the-dying-derbyshire-dialect

Local Dialects in Derbyshire: www.derbyshire.net/dialects

Derby Telegraph, 'Is "Ey up, mi duck" double Dutch?': www.thisisderbyshire.co.uk/Ey-mi-duck-double-Dutch-Christa/story-11597718-detail/story.html#axzz2NFl8wQ4h

Wikipedia, 'East Midlands English': http://en.wikipedia.org/wiki/East_Midlands_English

Other useful publications

Banks, F.R., *The Peak District*, Robert Hale and Company (1975)

Bellamy, Rex, *The Peak District Companion*, David and Charles (1981)

Bellhouse, Marguerite, *The History of Combs, My Village*, self-published (1968)

Bunting, W. Braylesford, *Chapel-en-le-Frith: Its History and its People*, Sherratt and Hughes (1940) (contains a short list of dialect words commonly used in Chapel-en-le-Frith and Peak Forest)

Christian, Roy, *Derbyshire*, Batsford (1978)

Gill, A.A., *A A Gill is Away*, Cassell & Co (2002)

Hey, David, '*Derbyshire: a History*, Carnegie Publishing (2008)

Hitchens, Ada, *The Warming Stone*, Caron Publications (1998)

Jewitt, Llewellyn, *The Ballads and Songs of Derbyshire*, Bemrose and Lothian (1867)

McMeeken, Louis, *Peak Place Names*, Halsgrove (2003)

Millward, R. and Robinson, A., *The Peak District*, Eyre Methuen (1975)

Porteous, Crichton, *Chuckling Joe*, Phoenix Press (1954)

Porteous, Crichton, *Derbyshire*, Robert Hale (1950) (includes a chapter entitled 'Reet Darbyshire')

Articles on Derbyshire Dialect

Daniel, Clarence, 'A Discussion of Derbyshire Dialect', *Derbyshire Life and Countryside* (March 1982)

Peach, Howard, 'East Derbyshire Dozen', *Derbyshire Life and Countryside* (December 2002)

Acknowledgements

Thanks are due to my wife Jo-Ann for all her help and advice during the preparation of this book and to the following people who have contributed material to the Dialect Dictionary: Edmund Bradbury, Nigel Bradbury, Jean Kadzewska, Mave Morrison, Jim Perkins and my daughter Charlotte Smith.

I am also grateful to F. Philip Holland, an authority on Derbyshire dialect and the author of *Words of the White Peak*, for kindly reading through the manuscript and offering helpful suggestions. Any errors of fact or interpretation are, of course, entirely my responsibility.

Photograph Credits

Joy Hales, the editor of *Derbyshire Life and Countryside*, kindly sourced the photograph of Crichton Porteous and gave permission for its use. Andrew McCloy, editor of the Bugle, contributed the photograph of the Youlgrave Silver Band, Derek Brumhead supplied a photograph of the Peak Forest Tramway and Michael Hunstone supplied the photograph of William and Advent Hunstone. The photograph of the Sherwood Foresters is reproduced with permission of the Buxton Advertiser and I am indebted to Keith Holford for sourcing the photograph of Buxworth Station. All other photographs used in this publication are from the author's own collection or from Picture the Past, an invaluable online archive of 100,000 (at the time of writing) historic images of people, places and events (www.picturethepast.org.uk), Derbyshire Record Office, Matlock DE4 3AG (01629 533809).